ARTEMIS TO ACTAEON
AND MORE: SELECTED VERSE

ARTEMIS TO ACTAEON AND MORE: SELECTED VERSE

EDITH WHARTON

WILDSIDE PRESS

ARTEMIS TO ACTAEON AND BEYOND: SELECTED VERSE

CONTENTS

PART IV

Part I

ARTEMIS TO ACTAEON

THOU couldst not look on me and live: so runs
The mortal legend—thou that couldst not live
Nor look on me (so the divine decree)!
That saw'st me in the cloud, the wave, the bough,
The clod commoved with April, and the shapes
Lurking 'twixt lid and eye-ball in the dark.
Mocked I thee not in every guise of life,
Hid in girls' eyes, a naiad in her well,
Wooed through their laughter, and like echo fled,
Luring thee down the primal silences
Where the heart hushes and the flesh is dumb?
Nay, was not I the tide that drew thee out
Relentlessly from the detaining shore,
Forth from the home-lights and the hailing voices,
Forth from the last faint headland's failing line,
Till I enveloped thee from verge to verge
And hid thee in the hollow of my being?
And still, because between us hung the veil,
The myriad-tinted veil of sense, thy feet
Refused their rest, thy hands the gifts of life,
Thy heart its losses, lest some lesser face
Should blur mine image in thine upturned soul
Ere death had stamped it there. This was thy thought.
And mine?

The gods, they say, have all: not so!
This have they—flocks on every hill, the blue
Spirals of incense and the amber drip
Of lucid honey-comb on sylvan shrines,
First-chosen weanlings, doves immaculate,
Twin-cooing in the osier-plaited cage,
And ivy-garlands glaucous with the dew:
Man's wealth, man's servitude, but not himself!
And so they pale, for lack of warmth they wane,
Freeze to the marble of their images,
And, pinnacled on man's subserviency,
Through the thick sacrificial haze discern
Unheeding lives and loves, as some cold peak
Through icy mists may enviously descry

Warm vales unzoned to the all-fruitful sun.
So they along an immortality
Of endless-envistaed homage strain their gaze,
If haply some rash votary, empty-urned,
But light of foot, with all-adventuring hand,
Break rank, fling past the people and the priest,
Up the last step, on to the inmost shrine,
And there, the sacred curtain in his clutch,
Drop dead of seeing—while the others prayed!
Yes, this we wait for, this renews us, this
Incarnates us, pale people of your dreams,
Who are but what you make us, wood or stone,
Or cold chryselephantine hung with gems,
Or else the beating purpose of your life,
Your sword, your clay, the note your pipe pursues,
The face that haunts your pillow, or the light
Scarce visible over leagues of labouring sea!
O thus through use to reign again, to drink
The cup of peradventure to the lees,
For one dear instant disimmortalised
In giving immortality!
So dream the gods upon their listless thrones.
Yet sometimes, when the votary appears,
With death-affronting forehead and glad eyes,
Too young, they rather muse, *too frail thou art*,
And shall we rob some girl of saffron veil
And nuptial garland for so slight a thing?
And so to their incurious loves return.

Not so with thee; for some indeed there are
Who would behold the truth and then return
To pine among the semblances—but I
Divined in thee the questing foot that never
Revisits the cold hearth of yesterday
Or calls achievement home. I from afar
Beheld thee fashioned for one hour's high use,
Nor meant to slake oblivion drop by drop.
Long, long hadst thou inhabited my dreams,
Surprising me as harts surprise a pool,
Stealing to drink at midnight; I divined
Thee rash to reach the heart of life, and lie
Bosom to bosom in occasion's arms.

And said: *Because I love thee thou shalt die!*

For immortality is not to range
Unlimited through vast Olympian days,
Or sit in dull dominion over time;
But this—to drink fate's utmost at a draught,
Nor feel the wine grow stale upon the lip,
To scale the summit of some soaring moment,
Nor know the dulness of the long descent,
To snatch the crown of life and seal it up
Secure forever in the vaults of death!

And this was thine: to lose thyself in me,
Relive in my renewal, and become
The light of other lives, a quenchless torch
Passed on from hand to hand, till men are dust
And the last garland withers from my shrine.

LIFE

NAY, lift me to thy lips, Life, and once more
Pour the wild music through me—

I quivered in the reed-bed with my kind,
Rooted in Lethe-bank, when at the dawn
There came a groping shape of mystery
Moving among us, that with random stroke
Severed, and rapt me from my silent tribe,
Pierced, fashioned, lipped me, sounding for a voice,
Laughing on Lethe-bank—and in my throat
I felt the wing-beat of the fledgeling notes,
The bubble of godlike laughter in my throat.

Such little songs she sang,
Pursing her lips to fit the tiny pipe,
They trickled from me like a slender spring
That strings frail wood-growths on its crystal thread,
Nor dreams of glassing cities, bearing ships.
She sang, and bore me through the April world
Matching the birds, doubling the insect-hum
In the meadows, under the low-moving airs,
And breathings of the scarce-articulate air
When it makes mouths of grasses—but when the sky
Burst into storm, and took great trees for pipes,
She thrust me in her breast, and warm beneath
Her cloudy vesture, on her terrible heart,
I shook, and heard the battle.

But more oft,
Those early days, we moved in charmed woods,
Where once, at dusk, she piped against a faun,
And one warm dawn a tree became a nymph
Listening; and trembled; and Life laughed and passed.
And once we came to a great stream that bore
The stars upon its bosom like a sea,
And ships like stars; so to the sea we came.
And there she raised me to her lips, and sent
One swift pang through me; then refrained her hand,
And whispered: "Hear—" and into my frail flanks,

Into my bursting veins, the whole sea poured
Its spaces and its thunder; and I feared.

We came to cities, and Life piped on me
Low calls to dreaming girls,
In counting-house windows, through the chink of gold,
Flung cries that fired the captive brain of youth,
And made the heavy merchant at his desk
Curse us for a cracked hurdy-gurdy; Life
Mimicked the hurdy-gurdy, and we passed.

We climbed the slopes of solitude, and there
Life met a god, who challenged her and said:
"Thy pipe against my lyre!" But "Wait!" she laughed,
And in my live flank dug a finger-hole,
And wrung new music from it. Ah, the pain!

We climbed and climbed, and left the god behind.
We saw the earth spread vaster than the sea,
With infinite surge of mountains surfed with snow,
And a silence that was louder than the deep;
But on the utmost pinnacle Life again
Hid me, and I heard the terror in her hair.

Safe in new vales, I ached for the old pang,
And clamoured "Play me against a god again!"
"Poor Marsyas-mortal—he shall bleed thee yet,"
She breathed and kissed me, stilling the dim need.
But evermore it woke, and stabbed my flank
With yearnings for new music and new pain.
"Another note against another god!"
I clamoured; and she answered: "Bide my time.
Of every heart-wound I will make a stop,
And drink thy life in music, pang by pang,
But first thou must yield the notes I stored in thee
At dawn beside the river. Take my lips."

She kissed me like a lover, but I wept,
Remembering that high song against the god,
And the old songs slept in me, and I was dumb.

*   *   *

We came to cavernous foul places, blind
With harpy-wings, and sulphurous with the glare
Of sinful furnaces—where hunger toiled,
And pleasure gathered in a starveling prey,
And death fed delicately on young bones.

"Now sing!" cried Life, and set her lips to me.
"Here are gods also. Wilt thou pipe for Dis?"
My cry was drowned beneath the furnace roar,
Choked by the sulphur-fumes; and beast-lipped gods
Laughed down on me, and mouthed the flutes of hell.

"Now sing!" said Life, reissuing to the stars;
And wrung a new note from my wounded side.

So came we to clear spaces, and the sea.
And now I felt its volume in my heart,
And my heart waxed with it, and Life played on me
The song of the Infinite. "Now the stars," she said.

Then from the utmost pinnacle again
She poured me on the wild sidereal stream,
And I grew with her great breathings, till we swept
The interstellar spaces like new worlds
Loosed from the fiery ruin of a star.

Cold, cold we rested on black peaks again,
Under black skies, under a groping wind;
And Life, grown old, hugged me to a numb breast,
Pressing numb lips against me. Suddenly
A blade of silver severed the black peaks
From the black sky, and earth was born again,
Breathing and various, under a god's feet.
A god! A god! I felt the heart of Life
Leap under me, and my cold flanks shook again.
He bore no lyre, he rang no challenge out,
But Life warmed to him, warming me with her,
And as he neared I felt beneath her hands
The stab of a new wound that sucked my soul
Forth in a new song from my throbbing throat.

*   *   *

"His name—his name?" I whispered, but she shed
The music faster, and I grew with it,
Became a part of it, while Life and I
Clung lip to lip, and I from her wrung song
As she from me, one song, one ecstasy,
In indistinguishable union blent,
Till she became the flute and I the player.
And lo! the song I played on her was more
Than any she had drawn from me; it held
The stars, the peaks, the cities, and the sea,
The faun's catch, the nymph's tremor, and the heart
Of dreaming girls, of toilers at the desk,
Apollo's challenge on the sunrise slope,
And the hiss of the night-gods mouthing flutes of hell—
All, to the dawn-wind's whisper in the reeds,
When Life first came, a shape of mystery,
Moving among us, and with random stroke
Severed, and rapt me from my silent tribe.
All this I wrung from her in that deep hour,
While Love stood murmuring: "Play the god, poor grass!"

Now, by that hour, I am a mate to thee
Forever, Life, however spent and clogged,
And tossed back useless to my native mud!
Yea, groping for new reeds to fashion thee
New instruments of anguish and delight,
Thy hand shall leap to me, thy broken reed,
Thine ear remember me, thy bosom thrill
With the old subjection, then when Love and I
Held thee, and fashioned thee, and made thee dance
Like a slave-girl to her pipers—yea, thou yet
Shalt hear my call, and dropping all thy toys
Thou'lt lift me to thy lips, Life, and once more
Pour the wild music through me—

VESALIUS IN ZANTE¹ (1564)

SET wide the window. Let me drink the day.
I loved light ever, light in eye and brain—
No tapers mirrored in long palace floors,
Nor dedicated depths of silent aisles,
But just the common dusty wind-blown day
That roofs earth's millions.

O, too long I walked
In that thrice-sifted air that princes breathe,
Nor felt the heaven-wide jostling of the winds
And all the ancient outlawry of earth!
Now let me breathe and see.

1 Vesalius, the great anatomist, studied at Louvain and Paris, and was
called by Venice to the chair of surgery in the University of Padua. He
was one of the first physiologists to dissect the human body, and his
great work "The Structure of the Human Body" was an open attack on
the physiology of Galen. The book excited such violent opposition, not
only in the Church but in the University, that in a fit of discouragement
he burned his remaining manuscripts and accepted the post of physi-
cian at the Court of Charles V., and afterward of his son, Philip II, of
Spain. This closed his life of free enquiry, for the Inquisition forbade all
scientific research, and the dissection of corpses was prohibited in
Spain. Vesalius led for many years the life of the rich and successful
court physician, but regrets for his past were never wholly extin-
guished, and in 1561 they were roused afresh by the reading of an ana-
tomical treatise by Gabriel Fallopius, his successor in the chair at
Padua. From that moment life in Spain became intolerable to Vesalius,
and in 1563 he set out for the East. Tradition reports that this journey
was a penance to which the Church condemned him for having opened
the body of a woman before she was actually dead; but more probably
Vesalius, sick of his long servitude, made the pilgrimage a pretext to es-
cape from Spain.

Fallopius had meanwhile died, and the Venetian Senate is said to have
offered Vesalius his old chair; but on the way home from Jerusalem he
was seized with illness, and died at Zante in 1564.

This pilgrimage
They call a penance—let them call it that!
I set my face to the East to shrive my soul
Of mortal sin? So be it. If my blade
Once questioned living flesh, if once I tore
The pages of the Book in opening it,
See what the torn page yielded ere the light
Had paled its buried characters—and judge!

The girl they brought me, pinioned hand and foot
In catalepsy—say I should have known
That trance had not yet darkened into death,
And held my scalpel. Well, suppose I *knew?*
Sum up the facts—her life against her death.
Her life? The scum upon the pools of pleasure
Breeds such by thousands. And her death? Perchance
The obolus to appease the ferrying Shade,
And waft her into immortality.
Think what she purchased with that one heart-flutter
That whispered its deep secret to my blade!
For, just because her bosom fluttered still,
It told me more than many rifled graves;
Because I spoke too soon, she answered me,
Her vain life ripened to this bud of death
As the whole plant is forced into one flower,
All her blank past a scroll on which God wrote
His word of healing—so that the poor flesh,
Which spread death living, died to purchase life!

Ah, no! The sin I sinned was mine, not theirs.
Not *that* they sent me forth to wash away—
None of their tariffed frailties, but a deed
So far beyond their grasp of good or ill
That, set to weigh it in the Church's balance,
Scarce would they know which scale to cast it in.
But I, I know. I sinned against my will,
Myself, my soul—the God within the breast:
Can any penance wash such sacrilege?

When I was young in Venice, years ago,
I walked the hospice with a Spanish monk,
A solitary cloistered in high thoughts,

17

The great Loyola, whom I reckoned then
A mere refurbisher of faded creeds,
Expert to edge anew the arms of faith,
As who should say, a Galenist, resolved
To hold the walls of dogma against fact,
Experience, insight, his own self, if need be!
Ah, how I pitied him, mine own eyes set
Straight in the level beams of Truth, who groped
In error's old deserted catacombs
And lit his tapers upon empty graves!
Ay, but he held his own, the monk—more man
Than any laurelled cripple of the wars,
Charles's spent shafts; for what he willed he willed,
As those do that forerun the wheels of fate,
Not take their dust—that force the virgin hours,

Hew life into the likeness of themselves
And wrest the stars from their concurrences.
So firm his mould; but mine the ductile soul
That wears the livery of circumstance
And hangs obsequious on its suzerain's eye.
For who rules now? The twilight-flitting monk,
Or I, that took the morning like an Alp?
He held his own, I let mine slip from me,
The birthright that no sovereign can restore;
And so ironic Time beholds us now
Master and slave—he lord of half the earth,
I ousted from my narrow heritage.

For there's the sting! My kingdom knows me not.
Reach me that folio—my usurper's title!
Fallopius reigning, *vice*—nay, not so:
Successor, not usurper. I am dead.
My throne stood empty; he was heir to it.
Ay, but who hewed his kingdom from the waste,
Cleared, inch by inch, the acres for his sowing,
Won back for man that ancient fief o' the Church,
His body? Who flung Galen from his seat,
And founded the great dynasty of truth
In error's central kingdom?

                    *   *   *

Ask men that,
And see their answer: just a wondering stare
To learn things were not always as they are—
The very fight forgotten with the fighter;
Already grows the moss upon my grave!
Ay, and so meet—hold fast to that, Vesalius.
They only, who re-conquer day by day
The inch of ground they camped on over-night,
Have right of foothold on this crowded earth.
I left mine own; he seized it; with it went
My name, my fame, my very self, it seems,
Till I am but the symbol of a man,
The sign-board creaking o'er an empty inn.
He names me—true! *Oh, give the door its due*
I entered by. Only, I pray you, note,
Had door been none, a shoulder-thrust of mine
Had breached the crazy wall"—he seems to say.
So meet—and yet a word of thanks, of praise,
Of recognition that the clue was found,
Seized, followed, clung to, by some hand now dust—
Had this obscured his quartering of my shield?

How the one weakness stirs again! I thought
I had done with that old thirst for gratitude
That lured me to the desert years ago.
I did my work—and was not that enough?
No; but because the idlers sneered and shrugged,
The envious whispered, the traducers lied,
And friendship doubted where it should have cheered
I flung aside the unfinished task, sought praise
Outside my soul's esteem, and learned too late
That victory, like God's kingdom, is within.
(Nay, let the folio rest upon my knee.
I do not feel its weight.) Ingratitude?
The hurrying traveller does not ask the name
Of him who points him on his way; and this
Fallopius sits in the mid-heart of me,
Because he keeps his eye upon the goal,
Cuts a straight furrow to the end in view,
Cares not who oped the fountain by the way,
But drinks to draw fresh courage for his journey.
That was the lesson that Ignatius taught—

The one I might have learned from him, but would not—
That we are but stray atoms on the wind,
A dancing transiency of summer eves,
Till we become one with our purpose, merged
In that vast effort of the race which makes
Mortality immortal.

"He that loseth
His life shall find it": so the Scripture runs.
But I so hugged the fleeting self in me,
So loved the lovely perishable hours,
So kissed myself to death upon their lips,
That on one pyre we perished in the end—
A grimmer bonfire than the Church e'er lit!
Yet all was well—or seemed so—till I heard
That younger voice, an echo of my own,
And, like a wanderer turning to his home,
Who finds another on the hearth, and learns,
Half-dazed, that other is his actual self
In name and claim, as the whole parish swears,
So strangely, suddenly, stood dispossessed
Of that same self I had sold all to keep,
A baffled ghost that none would see or hear!
"Vesalius? Who's Vesalius? This Fallopius
It is who dragged the Galen-idol down,
Who rent the veil of flesh and forced a way
Into the secret fortalice of life"—
Yet it was I that bore the brunt of it!

Well, better so! Better awake and live
My last brief moment as the man I was,
Than lapse from life's long lethargy to death
Without one conscious interval. At least
I repossess my past, am once again
No courtier med'cining the whims of kings
In muffled palace-chambers, but the free
Friendless Vesalius, with his back to the wall
And all the world against him. O, for that
Best gift of all, Fallopius, take my thanks—
That, and much more. At first, when Padua wrote:
"Master, Fallopius dead, resume again
The chair even he could not completely fill,

And see what usury age shall take of youth
In honours forfeited"—why, just at first,
I was quite simply credulously glad
To think the old life stood ajar for me,
Like a fond woman's unforgetting heart.
But now that death waylays me—now I know
This isle is the circumference of my days,
And I shall die here in a little while—
So also best, Fallopius!

For I see
The gods may give anew, but not restore;
And though I think that, in my chair again,
I might have argued my supplanters wrong
In this or that—this Cesalpinus, say,
With all his hot-foot blundering in the dark,
Fabricius, with his over-cautious clutch
On Galen (systole and diastole
Of Truth's mysterious heart!)—yet, other ways,
It may be that this dying serves the cause.
For Truth stays not to build her monument
For this or that co-operating hand,
But props it with her servants' failures—nay,
Cements its courses with their blood and brains,
A living substance that shall clinch her walls
Against the assaults of time. Already, see,
Her scaffold rises on my hidden toil,
I but the accepted premiss whence must spring
The airy structure of her argument;
Nor could the bricks it rests on serve to build
The crowning finials. I abide her law:
A different substance for a different end—
Content to know I hold the building up;
Though men, agape at dome and pinnacles,
Guess not, the whole must crumble like a dream
But for that buried labour underneath.
Yet, Padua, I had still my word to say!
Let others say it!—Ah, but will they guess
Just the one word—? Nay, Truth is many-tongued.
What one man failed to speak, another finds
Another word for. May not all converge
In some vast utterance, of which you and I,

Fallopius, were but halting syllables?
So knowledge come, no matter how it comes!
No matter whence the light falls, so it fall!
Truth's way, not mine—that I, whose service failed
In action, yet may make amends in praise.
Fabricius, Cesalpinus, say your word,
Not yours, or mine, but Truth's, as you receive it!
You miss a point I saw? See others, then!
Misread my meaning? Yet expound your own!
Obscure one space I cleared? The sky is wide,
And you may yet uncover other stars.
For thus I read the meaning of this end:
There are two ways of spreading light: to be
The candle or the mirror that reflects it.
I let my wick burn out—there yet remains
To spread an answering surface to the flame
That others kindle.

Turn me in my bed.
The window darkens as the hours swing round;
But yonder, look, the other casement glows!
Let me face westward as my sun goes down.

MARGARET OF CORTONA

FRA PAOLO, since they say the end is near,
And you of all men have the gentlest eyes,
Most like our father Francis; since you know
How I have toiled and prayed and scourged and striven,
Mothered the orphan, waked beside the sick,
Gone empty that mine enemy might eat,
Given bread for stones in famine years, and channelled
With vigilant knees the pavement of this cell,
Till I constrained the Christ upon the wall
To bend His thorn-crowned Head in mute forgiveness . . .
Three times He bowed it . . . (but the whole stands writ,
Sealed with the Bishop's signet, as you know),
Once for each person of the Blessed Three—
A miracle that the whole town attests,
The very babes thrust forward for my blessing,
And either parish plotting for my bones—
Since this you know: sit near and bear with me.

I have lain here, these many empty days
I thought to pack with Credos and Hail Marys
So close that not a fear should force the door—
But still, between the blessed syllables
That taper up like blazing angel heads,
Praise over praise, to the Unutterable,
Strange questions clutch me, thrusting fiery arms,
As though, athwart the close-meshed litanies,
My dead should pluck at me from hell, with eyes
Alive in their obliterated faces! . . .
I have tried the saints' names and our blessed Mother's
Fra Paolo, I have tried them o'er and o'er,
And like a blade bent backward at first thrust
They yield and fail me—and the questions stay.
And so I thought, into some human heart,
Pure, and yet foot-worn with the tread of sin,
If only I might creep for sanctuary,
It might be that those eyes would let me rest. . .

Fra Paolo, listen. How should I forget
The day I saw him first? (You know the one.)

I had been laughing in the market-place
With others like me, I the youngest there,
Jostling about a pack of mountebanks
Like flies on carrion (I the youngest there!),
Till darkness fell; and while the other girls
Turned this way, that way, as perdition beckoned,
I, wondering what the night would bring, half hoping:
If not, this once, a child's sleep in my garret,
At least enough to buy that two-pronged coral
The others covet 'gainst the evil eye,
Since, after all, one sees that I'm the youngest—
So, muttering my litany to hell
(The only prayer I knew that was not Latin),
Felt on my arm a touch as kind as yours,
And heard a voice as kind as yours say "Come."
I turned and went; and from that day I never
Looked on the face of any other man.
So much is known; so much effaced; the sin
Cast like a plague-struck body to the sea,
Deep, deep into the unfathomable pardon—
(The Head bowed thrice, as the whole town attests).
What more, then? To what purpose? Bear with me!—

It seems that he, a stranger in the place,
First noted me that afternoon and wondered:
How grew so white a bud in such black slime,
And why not mine the hand to pluck it out?
Why, so Christ deals with souls, you cry—what then?
Not so! Not so! When Christ, the heavenly gardener,
Plucks flowers for Paradise (do I not know?),
He snaps the stem above the root, and presses
The ransomed soul between two convent walls,
A lifeless blossom in the Book of Life.
But when my lover gathered me, he lifted
Stem, root and all—ay, and the clinging mud—
And set me on his sill to spread and bloom
After the common way, take sun and rain,
And make a patch of brightness for the street,
Though raised above rough fingers—so you make
A weed a flower, and others, passing, think:
"Next ditch I cross, I'll lift a root from it,
And dress my window" . . . and the blessing spreads.

Well, so I grew, with every root and tendril
Grappling the secret anchorage of his love,
And so we loved each other till he died. . . .

Ah, that black night he left me, that dead dawn
I found him lying in the woods, alive
To gasp my name out and his life-blood with it,
As though the murderer's knife had probed for me
In his hacked breast and found me in each wound. . .
Well, it was there Christ came to me, you know,
And led me home—just as that other led me.
(*Just as that other?* Father, bear with me!)
My lover's death, they tell me, saved my soul,
And I have lived to be a light to men.
And gather sinners to the knees of grace.
All this, you say, the Bishop's signet covers.
But stay! Suppose my lover had not died?
(At last my question! Father, help me face it.)
I say: Suppose my lover had not died—
Think you I ever would have left him living,
Even to be Christ's blessed Margaret?
—We lived in sin? Why, to the sin I died to
That other was as Paradise, when God
Walks there at eventide, the air pure gold,
And angels treading all the grass to flowers!
He was my Christ—he led me out of hell—
He died to save me (so your casuists say!)—
Could Christ do more? Your Christ out-pity mine?
Why, *yours* but let the sinner bathe His feet;
Mine raised her to the level of his heart. . .
And then Christ's way is saving, as man's way
Is squandering—and the devil take the shards!
But this man kept for sacramental use
The cup that once had slaked a passing thirst;
This man declared: "The same clay serves to model
A devil or a saint; the scribe may stain
The same fair parchment with obscenities,
Or gild with benedictions; nay," he cried,
"Because a satyr feasted in this wood,
And fouled the grasses with carousing foot,
Shall not a hermit build his chapel here
And cleanse the echoes with his litanies?

The sodden grasses spring again—why not
The trampled soul? Is man less merciful
Than nature, good more fugitive than grass?"
And so—if, after all, he had not died,
And suddenly that door should know his hand,
And with that voice as kind as yours he said:
"Come, Margaret, forth into the sun again,
Back to the life we fashioned with our hands
Out of old sins and follies, fragments scorned
Of more ambitious builders, yet by Love,
The patient architect, so shaped and fitted
That not a crevice let the winter in—"
Think you my bones would not arise and walk,
This bruised body (as once the bruised soul)
Turn from the wonders of the seventh heaven
As from the antics of the market-place?
If this could be (as I so oft have dreamed),
I, who have known both loves, divine and human,
Think you I would not leave this Christ for that?

—I rave, you say? You start from me, Fra Paolo?
Go, then; your going leaves me not alone.
I marvel, rather, that I feared the question,
Since, now I name it, it draws near to me
With such dear reassurance in its eyes,
And takes your place beside me. . .

Nay, I tell you,
Fra Paolo, I have cried on all the saints—
If this be devil's prompting, let them drown it
In Alleluias! Yet not one replies.
And, for the Christ there—is He silent too?
Your Christ? Poor father; you that have but one,
And that one silent—how I pity you!
He will not answer? Will not help you cast
The devil out? But hangs there on the wall,
Blind wood and bone—?

How if *I* call on Him—
I, whom He talks with, as the town attests?
If ever prayer hath ravished me so high
That its wings failed and dropped me in Thy breast,

Christ, I adjure Thee! By that naked hour
Of innermost commixture, when my soul
Contained Thee as the paten holds the host,
Judge Thou alone between this priest and me;
Nay, rather, Lord, between my past and present,
Thy Margaret and that other's—whose she is
By right of salvage—and whose call should follow!
Thine? Silent still.—Or his, who stooped to her,
And drew her to Thee by the bands of love?
Not Thine? Then his?

Ah, Christ—the thorn-crowned Head
Bends . . . bends again . . . down on your knees,

Fra Paolo!
If his, then Thine!

Kneel, priest, for this is heaven. . .

A TORCHBEARER

GREAT cities rise and have their fall; the brass
That held their glories moulders in its turn.
Hard granite rots like an uprooted weed,
And ever on the palimpsest of earth
Impatient Time rubs out the word he writ.
But one thing makes the years its pedestal,
Springs from the ashes of its pyre, and claps
A skyward wing above its epitaph—
The will of man willing immortal things.

The ages are but baubles hung upon
The thread of some strong lives—and one slight wrist
May lift a century above the dust;
For Time,
The Sisyphean load of little lives,
Becomes the globe and sceptre of the great.
But who are these that, linking hand in hand,
Transmit across the twilight waste of years
The flying brightness of a kindled hour?
Not always, nor alone, the lives that search
How they may snatch a glory out of heaven
Or add a height to Babel; oftener they
That in the still fulfilment of each day's
Pacific order hold great deeds in leash,
That in the sober sheath of tranquil tasks
Hide the attempered blade of high emprise,
And leap like lightning to the clap of fate.

So greatly gave he, nurturing 'gainst the call
Of one rare moment all the daily store
Of joy distilled from the acquitted task,
And that deliberate rashness which bespeaks
The pondered action passed into the blood;
So swift to harden purpose into deed
That, with the wind of ruin in his hair,
Soul sprang full-statured from the broken flesh,
And at one stroke he lived the whole of life,
Poured all in one libation to the truth,
A brimming flood whose drops shall overflow

On deserts of the soul long beaten down
By the brute hoof of habit, till they spring
In manifold upheaval to the sun.

Call here no high artificer to raise
His wordy monument—such lives as these
Make death a dull misnomer and its pomp
An empty vesture. Let resounding lives
Re-echo splendidly through high-piled vaults
And make the grave their spokesman—such as he
Are as the hidden streams that, underground,
Sweeten the pastures for the grazing kine,
Or as spring airs that bring through prison bars
The scent of freedom; or a light that burns
Immutably across the shaken seas,
Forevermore by nameless hands renewed,
Where else were darkness and a glutted shore.

II

THE MORTAL LEASE

I

BECAUSE the currents of our love are poured
Through the slow welter of the primal flood
From some blind source of monster-haunted mud,
And flung together by random forces stored
Ere the vast void with rushing worlds was scored—
Because we know ourselves but the dim scud
Tossed from their heedless keels, the sea-blown bud
That wastes and scatters ere the wave has roared—

Because we have this knowledge in our veins,
Shall we deny the journey's gathered lore—
The great refusals and the long disdains,
The stubborn questing for a phantom shore,
The sleepless hopes and memorable pains,
And all mortality's immortal gains?

II

Because our kiss is as the moon to draw
The mounting waters of that red-lit sea
That circles brain with sense, and bids us be
The playthings of an elemental law,
Shall we forego the deeper touch of awe
On love's extremest pinnacle, where we,
Winging the vistas of infinity,
Gigantic on the mist our shadows saw?

Shall kinship with the dim first-moving clod
Not draw the folded pinion from the soul,
And shall we not, by spirals vision-trod,
Reach upward to some still-retreating goal,
As earth, escaping from the night's control,
Drinks at the founts of morning like a god?

III

All, all is sweet in that commingled draught
Mysterious, that life pours for lovers' thirst,
And I would meet your passion as the first
Wild woodland woman met her captor's craft,
Or as the Greek whose fearless beauty laughed
And doffed her raiment by the Attic flood;
But in the streams of my belated blood
Flow all the warring potions love has quaffed.

How can I be to you the nymph who danced
Smooth by Ilissus as the plane-tree's bole,
Or how the Nereid whose drenched lashes glanced
Like sea-flowers through the summer sea's long roll—
I that have also been the nun entranced
Who night-long held her Bridegroom in her soul?

IV

"Sad Immortality is dead," you say,
"And all her grey brood banished from the soul;
Life, like the earth, is now a rounded whole,
The orb of man's dominion. Live to-day."
And every sense in me leapt to obey,
Seeing the routed phantoms backward roll;
But from their waning throng a whisper stole,
And touched the morning splendour with decay.

"Sad Immortality is dead; and we
The funeral train that bear her to her grave.
Yet hath she left a two-faced progeny
In hearts of men, and some will always see
The skull beneath the wreath, yet always crave
In every kiss the folded kiss to be."

V

Yet for one rounded moment I will be
No more to you than what my lips may give,
And in the circle of your kisses live

As in some island of a storm-blown sea,
Where the cold surges of infinity
Upon the outward reefs unheeded grieve,
And the loud murmur of our blood shall weave
Primeval silences round you and me.

If in that moment we are all we are
We live enough. Let this for all requite.
Do I not know, some winged things from far
Are borne along illimitable night
To dance their lives out in a single flight
Between the moonrise and the setting star?

VI

The Moment came, with sacramental cup
Lifted—and all the vault of life grew bright
With tides of incommensurable light—
But tremblingly I turned and covered up
My face before the wonder. Down the slope
I heard her feet in irretrievable flight,
And when I looked again, my stricken sight
Saw night and rain in a dead world agrope.

Now walks her ghost beside me, whispering
With lips derisive: "Thou that wouldst forego—
What god assured thee that the cup I bring
Globes not in every drop the cosmic show,
All that the insatiate heart of man can wring
From life's long vintage?—Now thou shalt not know."

VII

Shall I not know? I, that could always catch
The sunrise in one beam along the wall,
The nests of June in April's mating call,
And ruinous autumn in the wind's first snatch
At summer's green impenetrable thatch—

That always knew far off the secret fall
Of a god's feet across the city's brawl,
The touch of silent fingers on my latch?

Not thou, vain Moment! Something more than thou
Shall write the score of what mine eyes have wept,
The touch of kisses that have missed my brow,
The murmur of wings that brushed me while I slept,
And some mute angel in the breast even now
Measures my loss by all that I have kept.

VIII

Strive we no more. Some hearts are like the bright
Tree-chequered spaces, flecked with sun and shade,
Where gathered in old days the youth and maid
To woo, and weave their dances: with the night
They cease their flutings, and the next day's light
Finds the smooth green unconscious of their tread,
And ready its velvet pliancies to spread
Under fresh feet, till these in turn take flight.

But other hearts a long long road doth span,
From some far region of old works and wars,
And the weary armies of the thoughts of man
Have trampled it, and furrowed it with scars,
And sometimes, husht, a sacred caravan
Moves over it alone, beneath the stars.

EXPERIENCE

I

LIKE Crusoe with the bootless gold we stand
Upon the desert verge of death, and say:
"What shall avail the woes of yesterday
To buy to-morrow's wisdom, in the land
Whose currency is strange unto our hand?
In life's small market they had served to pay
Some late-found rapture, could we but delay
Till Time hath matched our means to our demand."

But otherwise Fate wills it, for, behold,
Our gathered strength of individual pain,
When Time's long alchemy hath made it gold,
Dies with us—hoarded all these years in vain,
Since those that might be heir to it the mould
Renew, and coin themselves new griefs again.

II

O Death, we come full-handed to thy gate,
Rich with strange burden of the mingled years,
Gains and renunciations, mirth and tears,
And love's oblivion, and remembering hate.
Nor know we what compulsion laid such freight
Upon our souls—and shall our hopes and fears
Buy nothing of thee, Death? Behold our wares,
And sell us the one joy for which we wait.
Had we lived longer, life had such for sale,
With the last coin of sorrow purchased cheap,
But now we stand before thy shadowy pale,
And all our longings lie within thy keep—
Death, can it be the years shall naught avail?

"Not so," Death answered, "they shall purchase sleep."

GRIEF

I

ON immemorial altitudes august
Grief holds her high dominion. Bold the feet
That climb unblenching to that stern retreat
Whence, looking down, man knows himself but dust.
There lie the mightiest passions, earthward thrust
Beneath her regnant footstool, and there meet
Pale ghosts of buried longings that were sweet,
With many an abdicated "shall" and "must."

For there she rules omnipotent, whose will
Compels a mute acceptance of her chart;
Who holds the world, and lo! it cannot fill
Her mighty hand; who will be served apart
With uncommunicable rites, and still
Surrender of the undivided heart.

II

She holds the world within her mighty hand,
And lo! it is a toy for babes to toss,
And all its shining imagery but dross,
To those that in her awful presence stand;
As sun-confronting eagles o'er the land
That lies below, they send their gaze across
The common intervals of gain and loss,
And hope's infinitude without a strand.

But he who, on that lonely eminence,
Watches too long the whirling of the spheres
Through dim eternities, descending thence
The voices of his kind no longer hears,
And, blinded by the spectacle immense,
Journeys alone through all the after years.

CHARTRES

I

IMMENSE, august, like some Titanic bloom,
The mighty choir unfolds its lithic core,
Petalled with panes of azure, gules and or,
Splendidly lambent in the Gothic gloom,
And stamened with keen flamelets that illume
The pale high-altar. On the prayer-worn floor,
By worshippers innumerous thronged of yore,
A few brown crones, familiars of the tomb,
The stranded driftwood of Faith's ebbing sea—
For these alone the finials fret the skies,
The topmost bosses shake their blossoms free,
While from the triple portals, with grave eyes,
Tranquil, and fixed upon eternity,
The cloud of witnesses still testifies.

II

The crimson panes like blood-drops stigmatise
The western floor. The aisles are mute and cold.
A rigid fetich in her robe of gold,
The Virgin of the Pillar, with blank eyes,
Enthroned beneath her votive canopies,
Gathers a meagre remnant to her fold.
The rest is solitude; the church, grown old,
Stands stark and grey beneath the burning skies.
Well-nigh again its mighty framework grows
To be a part of nature's self, withdrawn
From hot humanity's impatient woes;
The floor is ridged like some rude mountain lawn,
And in the east one giant window shows
The roseate coldness of an Alp at dawn.

TWO BACKGROUNDS

I

LA VIERGE AU DONATEU

HERE by the ample river's argent sweep,
Bosomed in tilth and vintage to her walls,
A tower-crowned Cybele in armoured sleep
The city lies, fat plenty in her halls,
With calm parochial spires that hold in fee
The friendly gables clustered at their base,
And, equipoised o'er tower and market-place,
The Gothic minister's winged immensity;
And in that narrow burgh, with equal mood,
Two placid hearts, to all life's good resigned,
Might, from the altar to the lych-gate, find
Long years of peace and dreamless plenitude.

II

MONA LISA

Yon strange blue city crowns a scarped steep
No mortal foot hath bloodlessly essayed:
Dreams and illusions beacon from its keep.
But at the gate an Angel bares his blade;
And tales are told of those who thought to gain
At dawn its ramparts; but when evening fell
Far off they saw each fading pinnacle
Lit with wild lightnings from the heaven of pain;
Yet there two souls, whom life's perversities
Had mocked with want in plenty, tears in mirth,
Might meet in dreams, ungarmented of earth,
And drain Joy's awful chalice to the lees.

THE TOMB OF ILARIA GIUNIGI

ILARIA, thou that wert so fair and dear
That death would fain disown thee, grief made wise
With prophecy thy husband's widowed eyes,
And bade him call the master's art to rear
Thy perfect image on the sculptured bier,
With dreaming lids, hands laid in peaceful guise
Beneath the breast that seems to fall and rise,
And lips that at love's call should answer "Here!"

First-born of the Renascence, when thy soul
Cast the sweet robing of the flesh aside,
Into these lovelier marble limbs it stole,
Regenerate in art's sunrise clear and wide,
As saints who, having kept faith's raiment whole,
Change it above for garments glorified.

THE ONE GRIEF

ONE grief there is, the helpmeet of my heart,
That shall not from me till my days be sped,
That walks beside me in sunshine and in shade,
And hath in all my fortunes equal part.
At first I feared it, and would often start
Aghast to find it bending o'er my bed,
Till usage slowly dulled the edge of dread,
And one cold night I cried: *How warm thou art!*

Since then we two have travelled hand in hand,
And, lo, my grief has been interpreter
For me in many a fierce and alien land
Whose speech young Joy had failed to understand,
Plucking me tribute of red gold and myrrh
From desolate whirlings of the desert sand.

THE EUMENIDES

THINK you we slept within the Delphic bower,
What time our victim sought Apollo's grace?
Nay, drawn into ourselves, in that deep place
Where good and evil meet, we bode our hour.
For not inexorable is our power.
And we are hunted of the prey we chase,
Soonest gain ground on them that flee apace,
And draw temerity from hearts that cower.

Shuddering we gather in the house of ruth,
And on the fearful turn a face of fear,
But they to whom the ways of doom are clear
Not vainly named us the Eumenides.
Our feet are faithful in the paths of truth,
And in the constant heart we house at peace.

III

ORPHEUS

Love will make men dare to die for their beloved. . . Of this
Alcestis is a monument . . . for she was willing to lay down her
life for her husband . . . and so noble did this appear to the gods
that they granted her the privilege of returning to earth . . . but
Orpheus, the son of OEagrus, they sent empty away. . .

—PLATO: *The Symposium*

ORPHEUS the Harper, coming to the gate
Where the implacable dim warder sate,
Besought for parley with a shade within,
Dearer to him than life itself had been,
Sweeter than sunlight on Illyrian sea,
Or bloom of myrtle, or murmur of laden bee,
Whom lately from his unconsenting breast
The Fates, at some capricious blind behest,
Intolerably had reft—Eurydice,
Dear to the sunlight as Illyrian sea,
Sweet as the murmur of bees, or myrtle bloom—
And uncompanioned led her to the tomb.

There, solitary by the Stygian tide,
Strayed her dear feet, the shadow of his own,
Since, 'mid the desolate millions who have died,
Each phantom walks its crowded path alone;
And there her head, that slept upon his breast,
No more had such sweet harbour for its rest,
Nor her swift ear from those disvoiced throats
Could catch one echo of his living notes,
And, dreaming nightly of her pallid doom,
No solace had he of his own young bloom,
But yearned to pour his blood into her veins
And buy her back with unimagined pains.

To whom the Shepherd of the Shadows said:
"Yea, many thus would bargain for their dead;
But when they hear my fatal gateway clang
Life quivers in them with a last sweet pang.
They see the smoke of home above the trees,

44

The cordage whistles on the harbour breeze;
The beaten path that wanders to the shore
Grows dear because they shall not tread it more,
The dog that drowsing on their threshold lies
Looks at them with their childhood in his eyes,
And in the sunset's melancholy fall
They read a sunrise that shall give them all."

"Not thus am I," the Harper smiled his scorn.
"I see no path but those her feet have worn;
My roof-tree is the shadow of her hair,
And the light breaking through her long despair
The only sunrise that mine eyelids crave;
For doubly dead without me in the grave
Is she who, if my feet had gone before,
Had found life dark as death's abhorred shore."

The gate clanged on him, and he went his way
Amid the alien millions, mute and grey,
Swept like a cold mist down an unlit strand,
Where nameless wreckage gluts the stealthy sand,
Drift of the cockle-shells of hope and faith
Wherein they foundered on the rock of death.

So came he to the image that he sought
(Less living than her semblance in his thought),
Who, at the summons of his thrilling notes,
Drew back to life as a drowned creature floats
Back to the surface; yet no less is dead.
And cold fear smote him till she spoke and said:
"Art thou then come to lay thy lips on mine,
And pour thy life's libation out like wine?
Shall I, through thee, revisit earth again,
Traverse the shining sea, the fruitful plain,
Behold the house we dwelt in, lay my head
Upon the happy pillows of our bed,
And feel in dreams the pressure of thine arms
Kindle these pulses that no memory warms?
Nay: give me for a space upon thy breast
Death's shadowy substitute for rapture—rest;
Then join again the joyous living throng,
And give me life, but give it in thy song;

For only they that die themselves may give
Life to the dead: and I would have thee live."

Fear seized him closer than her arms; but he
Answered: "Not so—for thou shalt come with me!
I sought thee not that we should part again,
But that fresh joy should bud from the old pain;
And the gods, if grudgingly their gifts they make,
Yield all to them that without asking take."

"The gods," she said, "(so runs life's ancient lore)
Yield all man takes, but always claim their score.
The iron wings of the Eumenides
When heard far off seem but a summer breeze;
But me thou'lt have alive on earth again
Only by paying here my meed of pain.
Then lay on my cold lips the tender ghost
Of the dear kiss that used to warm them most,
Take from my frozen hands thy hands of fire,
And of my heart-strings make thee a new lyre,
That in thy music men may find my voice,
And something of me still on earth rejoice."

Shuddering he heard her, but with close-flung arm
Swept her resisting through the ghostly swarm.
"Swift, hide thee 'neath my cloak, that we may glide
Past the dim warder as the gate swings wide."
He whirled her with him, lighter than a leaf
Unwittingly whirled onward by a brief
Autumnal eddy; but when the fatal door
Suddenly yielded him to life once more,
And issuing to the all-consoling skies
He turned to seek the sunlight in her eyes,
He clutched at emptiness—she was not there;
And the dim warder answered to his prayer:
"Only once have I seen the wonder wrought.
But when Alcestis thus her master sought,
Living she sought him not, nor dreamed that fate
For any subterfuge would swing my gate.
Loving, she gave herself to livid death,
Joyous she bought his respite with her breath,
Came, not embodied, but a tenuous shade,

46

In whom her rapture a great radiance made.
For never saw I ghost upon this shore
Shine with such living ecstasy before,
Nor heard an exile from the light above
Hail me with smiles: *Thou art not Death but Love!*

"But when the gods, frustrated, this beheld,
How, living still, among the dead she dwelled,
Because she lived in him whose life she won,
And her blood beat in his beneath the sun,
They reasoned: 'When the bitter Stygian wave
The sweetness of love's kisses cannot lave,
When the pale flood of Lethe washes not
From mortal mind one high immortal thought,
Akin to us the earthly creature grows,
Since nature suffers only what it knows.
If she whom we to this grey desert banned
Still dreams she treads with him the sunlit land
That for his sake she left without a tear,
Set wide the gates—her being is not here.'

"So ruled the gods; but thou, that sought'st to give
Thy life for love, yet for thyself wouldst live.
They know not for their kin; but back to earth
Give, pitying, one that is of mortal birth."

Humbled the Harper heard, and turned away,
Mounting alone to the empoverished day;
Yet, as he left the Stygian shades behind,
He heard the cordage on the harbour wind,
Saw the blue smoke above the homestead trees,
And in his hidden heart was glad of these.

AN AUTUMN SUNSET

I

LEAGUERED in fire
The wild black promontories of the coast extend
Their savage silhouettes;
The sun in universal carnage sets,
And, halting higher,
The motionless storm-clouds mass their sullen threats,
Like an advancing mob in sword-points penned,
That, balked, yet stands at bay.
Mid-zenith hangs the fascinated day
In wind-lustrated hollows crystalline,
A wan Valkyrie whose wide pinions shine
Across the ensanguined ruins of the fray,
And in her hand swings high o'erhead,
Above the waste of war,
The silver torch-light of the evening star
Wherewith to search the faces of the dead.

II

Lagooned in gold,
Seem not those jetty promontories rather
The outposts of some ancient land forlorn,
Uncomforted of morn,
Where old oblivions gather,
The melancholy unconsoling fold
Of all things that go utterly to death
And mix no more, no more
With life's perpetually awakening breath?
Shall Time not ferry me to such a shore,
Over such sailless seas,
To walk with hope's slain importunities
In miserable marriage? Nay, shall not
All things be there forgot,
Save the sea's golden barrier and the black
Close-crouching promontories?
Dead to all shames, forgotten of all glories,

Shall I not wander there, a shadow's shade,
A spectre self-destroyed,
So purged of all remembrance and sucked back
Into the primal void,
That should we on that shore phantasmal meet
I should not know the coming of your feet?

MOONRISE OVER TYRINGHAM

NOW the high holocaust of hours is done,
And all the west empurpled with their death,
How swift oblivion drinks the fallen sun,
How little while the dusk remembereth!

Though some there were, proud hours that marched in mail,
And took the morning on auspicious crest,
Crying to fortune "Back, for I prevail!"—
Yet now they lie disfeatured with the rest;

And some that stole so soft on destiny
Methought they had surprised her to a smile;
But these fled frozen when she turned to see,
And moaned and muttered through my heart awhile.

But now the day is emptied of them all,
And night absorbs their life-blood at a draught;
And so my life lies, as the gods let fall
An empty cup from which their lips have quaffed.

Yet see—night is not . . . by translucent ways,
Up the grey void of autumn afternoon
Steals a mild crescent, charioted in haze,
And all the air is merciful as June.

The lake is a forgotten streak of day
That trembles through the hemlocks' darkling bars,
And still, my heart, still some divine delay
Upon the threshold holds the earliest stars.

O pale equivocal hour, whose suppliant feet
Haunt the mute reaches of the sleeping wind,
Art thou a watcher stealing to entreat
Prayer and sepulture for thy fallen kind?

Poor plaintive waif of a predestined race,
Their ruin gapes for thee. Why linger here?
Go hence in silence. Veil thine orphaned face,
Lest I should look on it and call it dear.

For if I love thee thou wilt sooner die;
Some sudden ruin will plunge upon thy head,
Midnight will fall from the revengeful sky
And hurl thee down among thy shuddering dead.

Avert thine eyes. Lapse softly from my sight,
Call not my name, nor heed if thine I crave,
So shalt thou sink through mitigated night
And bathe thee in the all-effacing wave.

But upward still thy perilous footsteps fare
Along a high-hung heaven drenched in light,
Dilating on a tide of crystal air
That floods the dark hills to their utmost height.

Strange hour, is this thy waning face that leans
Out of mid-heaven and makes my soul its glass?
What victory is imaged there? What means
Thy tarrying smile? Oh, veil thy lips and pass.

Nay . . . pause and let me name thee! For I see,
O with what flooding ecstasy of light,
Strange hour that wilt not loose thy hold on me,
Thou'rt not day's latest, but the first of night!

And after thee the gold-foot stars come thick,
From hand to hand they toss the flying fire,
Till all the zenith with their dance is quick
About the wheeling music of the Lyre.

Dread hour that lead'st the immemorial round,
With lifted torch revealing one by one
The thronging splendours that the day held bound,
And how each blue abyss enshrines its sun—

Be thou the image of a thought that fares
Forth from itself, and flings its ray ahead,
Leaping the barriers of ephemeral cares,
To where our lives are but the ages' tread,

And let this year be, not the last of youth,
But first—like thee!—of some new train of hours,
If more remote from hope, yet nearer truth,
And kin to the unpetitionable powers.

ALL SOULS

I

A THIN moon faints in the sky o'erhead,
And dumb in the churchyard lie the dead.
Walk we not, Sweet, by garden ways,
Where the late rose hangs and the phlox delays,
But forth of the gate and down the road,
Past the church and the yews, to their dim abode.
For it's turn of the year and All Souls' night,
When the dead can hear and the dead have sight.

II

Fear not that sound like wind in the trees:
It is only their call that comes on the breeze;
Fear not the shudder that seems to pass:
It is only the tread of their feet on the grass;
Fear not the drip of the bough as you stoop:
It is only the touch of their hands that grope—
For the year's on the turn and it's All Souls' night,
When the dead can yearn and the dead can smite.

III

And where should a man bring his sweet to woo
But here, where such hundreds were lovers too?
Where lie the dead lips that thirst to kiss,
The empty hands that their fellows miss,
Where the maid and her lover, from sere to green,
Sleep bed by bed, with the worm between?
For it's turn of the year and All Souls' night,
When the dead can hear and the dead have sight.

IV

And now they rise and walk in the cold,
Let us warm their blood and give youth to the old.
Let them see us and hear us, and say: "Ah, thus
In the prime of the year it went with us!"
Till their lips drawn close, and so long unkist,
Forget they are mist that mingles with mist!
For the year's on the turn, and it's All Souls' night,
When the dead can burn and the dead can smite.

V

Till they say, as they hear us—poor dead, poor dead!—
"Just an hour of this, and our age-long bed—
Just a thrill of the old remembered pains
To kindle a flame in our frozen veins,
A touch, and a sight, and a floating apart,
As the chill of dawn strikes each phantom heart—
For it's turn of the year and All Souls' night,
When the dead can hear and the dead have sight."

VI

And where should the living feel alive
But here in this wan white humming hive,
As the moon wastes down, and the dawn turns cold,
And one by one they creep back to the fold?
And where should a man hold his mate and say:
"One more, one more, ere we go their way"?
For the year's on the turn, and it's All Souls' night,
When the living can learn by the churchyard light.

VII

And how should we break faith who have seen
Those dead lips plight with the mist between,
And how forget, who have seen how soon
They lie thus chambered and cold to the moon?
How scorn, how hate, how strive, wee too,

Who must do so soon as those others do?
For it's All Souls' night, and break of the day,
And behold, with the light the dead are away. . .

ALL SAINTS

ALL so grave and shining see they come
From the blissful ranks of the forgiven,
Though so distant wheels the nearest crystal dome,
And the spheres are seven.

Are you in such haste to come to earth,
Shining ones, the Wonder on your brow,
To the low poor places of your birth,
And the day that must be darkness now?

Does the heart still crave the spot it yearned on
In the grey and mortal years,
The pure flame the smoky hearth it burned on,
The clear eye its tears?

Was there, in the narrow range of living,
After all the wider scope?
In the old old rapture of forgiving,
In the long long flight of hope?

Come you, from free sweep across the spaces,
To the irksome bounds of mortal law,
From the all-embracing Vision, to some face's
Look that never saw?

Never we, imprisoned here, had sought you,
Lured you with the ancient bait of pain,
Down the silver current of the light-years brought you
To the beaten round again—

Is it you, perchance, who ache to strain us
Dumbly to the dim transfigured breast,
Or with tragic gesture would detain us
From the age-long search for rest?

Is the labour then more glorious than the laurel,
The learning than the conquered thought?
Is the meed of men the righteous quarrel,
Not the justice wrought?

Long ago we guessed it, faithful ghosts,
Proudly chose the present for our scene,
And sent out indomitable hosts
Day by day to widen our demesne.

Sit you by our hearth-stone, lone immortals,
Share again the bitter wine of life!
Well we know, beyond the peaceful portals
There is nothing better than our strife,

Nought more thrilling than the cry that calls us,
Spent and stumbling, to the conflict vain,
After each disaster that befalls us
Nerves us for a sterner strain.

And, when flood or foeman shakes the sleeper
In his moment's lapse from pain,
Bids us fold our tents, and flee our kin, and deeper
Drive into the wilderness again.

THE OLD POLE STAR

BEFORE the clepsydra had bound the days
Man tethered Change to his fixed star, and said:
"The elder races, that long since are dead,
Marched by that light; it swerves not from its base
Though all the worlds about it wax and fade."

When Egypt saw it, fast in reeling spheres,
Her Pyramids shaft-centred on its ray
She reared and said: "Long as this star holds sway
In uninvaded ether, shall the years
Revere my monuments—" and went her way.

The Pyramids abide; but through the shaft
That held the polar pivot, eye to eye,
Look now—blank nothingness! As though Change laughed
At man's presumption and his puny craft,
The star has slipped its leash and roams the sky.

Yet could the immemorial piles be swung
A skyey hair's-breadth from their rooted base,
Back to the central anchorage of space,
Ah, then again, as when the race was young,
Should they behold the beacon of the race!

Of old, men said: "The Truth is there: we rear
Our faith full-centred on it. It was known
Thus of the elders who foreran us here,
Mapped out its circuit in the shifting sphere,
And found it, 'mid mutation, fixed alone."

Change laughs again, again the sky is cold,
And down that fissure now no star-beam glides.
Yet they whose sweep of vision grows not old
Still at the central point of space behold
Another pole-star: for the Truth abides.

A GRAVE

THOUGH life should come
With all its marshalled honours, trump and drum,
To proffer you the captaincy of some
Resounding exploit, that shall fill
Man's pulses with commemorative thrill,
And be a banner to far battle days
For truths unrisen upon untrod ways,
What would your answer be,
O heart once brave?
Seek otherwhere; for me,
I watch beside a grave.

Though to some shining festival of thought
The sages call you from steep citadel
Of bastioned argument, whose rampart gained
Yields the pure vision passionately sought,
In dreams known well,
But never yet in wakefulness attained,
How should you answer to their summons, save:
I watch beside a grave?

Though Beauty, from her fane within the soul
Of fire-tongued seers descending,
Or from the dream-lit temples of the past
With feet immortal wending,
Illuminate grief's antre swart and vast
With half-veiled face that promises the whole
To him who holds her fast,
What answer could you give?
Sight of one face I crave,
One only while I live;
Woo elsewhere; for I watch beside a grave.

Though love of the one heart that loves you best,
A storm-tossed messenger,
Should beat its wings for shelter in your breast,
Where clung its last year's nest,
The nest you built together and made fast
Lest envious winds should stir,

And winged each delicate thought to minister
With sweetness far-amassed
To the young dreams within—
What answer could it win?
The nest was whelmed in sorrow's rising wave,
Nor could I reach one drowning dream to save,
I watch beside a grave.

NON DOLET!

AGE after age the fruit of knowledge falls
To ashes on men's lips;
Love fails, faith sickens, like a dying tree
Life sheds its dreams that no new spring recalls;
The longed-for ships
Come empty home or founder on the deep,
And eyes first lose their tears and then their sleep.

So weary a world it lies, forlorn of day,
And yet not wholly dark,
Since evermore some soul that missed the mark
Calls back to those agrope
In the mad maze of hope,
"Courage, my brothers—I have found the way!"

The day is lost? What then?
What though the straggling rear-guard of the fight
Be whelmed in fear and night,
And the flying scouts proclaim
That death has gripped the van—
Ever the heart of man
Cheers on the hearts of men!

"It hurts not!" dying cried the Roman wife;
And one by one
The leaders in the strife
Fall on the blade of failure and exclaim:
"The day is won!"

A HUNTING-SONG

HUNTERS, where does Hope nest?
Not in the half-oped breast,
Nor the young rose,
Nor April sunrise—those
With a quick wing she brushes,
The wide world through,
Greets with the throat of thrushes,
Fades from as fast as dew.

But, would you spy her sleeping,
Cradled warm,
Look in the breast of weeping,
The tree stript by storm;
But, would you bind her fast,
Yours at last,
Bed-mate and lover,
Gain the last headland bare
That the cold tides cover,
There may you capture her, there,
Where the sea gives to the ground
Only the drift of the drowned.
Yet, if she slips you, once found,
Push to her uttermost lair
In the low house of despair.
There will she watch by your head,
Sing to you till you be dead,
Then, with your child in her breast,
In another heart build a new nest.

SURVIVAL

WHEN you and I, like all things kind or cruel,
The garnered days and light evasive hours,
Are gone again to be a part of flowers
And tears and tides, in life's divine renewal,

If some grey eve to certain eyes should wear
A deeper radiance than mere light can give,
Some silent page abruptly flush and live,
May it not be that you and I are there?

USES

AH, from the niggard tree of Time
How quickly fall the hours!
It needs no touch of wind or rime
To loose such facile flowers.

Drift of the dead year's harvesting,
They clog to-morrow's way,
Yet serve to shelter growths of spring
Beneath their warm decay,

Or, blent by pious hands with rare
Sweet savours of content,
Surprise the soul's December air
With June's forgotten scent.

A MEETING

ON a sheer peak of joy we meet;
Below us hums the abyss;
Death either way allures our feet
If we take one step amiss.

One moment let us drink the blue
Transcendent air together—
Then down where the same old work's to do
In the same dull daily weather.

We may not wait . . . yet look below!
How part? On this keen ridge
But one may pass. They call you—go!
My life shall be your bridge.

IV

THE PARTING DAY

I.

SOME busy hands have brought to light,
And laid beneath my eye,
The dress I wore that afternoon
You came to say good-by.

About it still there seems to cling
Some fragrance unexpressed,
The ghostly odor of the rose
I wore upon my breast;

And, subtler than all flower-scent,
The sacred garment holds
The memory of that parting day
Close hidden in its folds.

The rose is dead, and you are gone,
But to the dress I wore
The rose's smell, the thought of you,
Are wed forevermore.

II.

That day you came to say good-by
(A month ago! It seems a year!)
How calm I was! I met your eye,
And in my own you saw no tear.

You heard me laugh and talk and jest,
And lightly grieve that you should go;
You saw the rose upon my breast,
But not the breaking heart below.

And when you came and took my hand,
It scarcely fluttered in your hold.
Alas, you did not understand!
For you were blind, and I was cold.

And now you cannot see my tears,
And now you cannot hear my cry.
A month ago? Nay, years and years
Have aged my heart since that good-by.

AEROPAGUS

WHERE suns chase suns in rhythmic dance,
Where seeds are springing from the dust,
Where mind sways mind with spirit-glance,
High court is held, and law is just.

No hill alone, a sovereign bar;
Through space the fiery sparks are whirled
That draw and cling, and shape a star,—
That burn and cool, and form a world

Whose hidden forces hear a voice
That leads them by a perfect plan:
"Obey," it cries, "with steadfast choice,
Law shall complete what law began.

"Refuse,—behold the broken arc,
The sky of all its stars despoiled;
The new germ smothered in the dark,
The snow-pure soul with sin assoiled."

The voice still saith, "While atoms weave
Both world and soul for utmost joy,
Who sins must suffer,—no reprieve;
The law that quickens must destroy."

A FAILURE

(She Speaks.)

I MEANT to be so strong and true!
The world may smile and question, When?
But what I might have been to you
I cannot be to other men.
Just one in twenty to the rest,
And all in all to you alone,—
This was my dream; perchance 'tis best
That this, like other dreams, is flown.

For you I should have been so kind,
So prompt my spirit to control,
To win fresh vigor for my mind,
And purer beauties for my soul;
Beneath your eye I might have grown
To that divine, ideal height,
Which, mating wholly with your own,
Our equal spirits should unite.

PATIENCE

PATIENCE and I have traveled hand in hand
So many days that I have grown to trace
The lines of sad, sweet beauty in her face,
And all its veiled depths to understand.

Not beautiful is she to eyes profane;
Silent and unrevealed her holy charms;
But, like a mother's, her serene, strong arms
Uphold my footsteps on the path of pain.

I long to cry,—her soft voice whispers, "Nay!"
I seek to fly, but she restrains my feet;
In wisdom stern, yet in compassion sweet,
She guides my helpless wanderings, day by day.

O my Beloved, life's golden visions fade,
And one by one life's phantom joys depart;
They leave a sudden darkness in the heart,
And patience fills their empty place instead.

WANTS

WE women want to many things;
And first we call for happiness,—
The careless boon the hour brings,
The smile, the song, and the caress.

And when the fancy fades, we cry,
Nay, give us one on whom to spend
Our heart's desire! When Love goes by
With folded wings, we seek a friend.

And then our children come, to prove
Our hearts but slumbered, and can wake;
And when they go, we're fain to love
Some other woman's for their sake.

But when both love and friendship fail,
We cry for duty, work to do;
Some end to gain beyond the pale
Of self, some height to journey to.

And then, before our task is done,
With sudden weariness oppressed,
We leave the shining goal unwon
And only ask for rest.

THE LAST GIUSTIANINI

O WIFE, wife, wife! As if the sacred name
Could weary one with saying! Once again
Laying against my brow your lips' soft flame,
Join with me, Sweetest, in love's new refrain,
Since the whole music of my late-found life
Is that we call each other "husband—wife."

And yet, stand back, and let your cloth of gold
Straighten its sumptuous lines from waist to knee,
And, flowing firmly outward, fold on fold,
Invest your slim young form with majesty
As when, in those calm bridal robes arrayed,
You stood beside me, and I was afraid.

I was afraid—O sweetness, whiteness, youth,
Best gift of God, I feared you! I, indeed,
For whom all womanhood has been, forsooth,
Summed up in the sole Virgin of the Creed,
I thought that day our Lady's self stood there
And bound herself to me with vow and prayer.

Ah, yes, that day. I sat, remember well,
Half-crook'd above a missal, and laid in
The gold-leaf slowly; silence in my cell;
The picture, Satan tempting Christ to sin
Upon the mount's blue, pointed pinnacle,
The world outspread beneath as fair as hell—

When suddenly they summoned me. I stood
Abashed before the Abbot, who reclined
Full-bellied in his chair beneath the rood,
And roseate with having lately dined;
And then—I standing there abashed—he said:
"The house of Giustiniani all lie dead."

It scarcely seemed to touch me (I had led
A grated life so long) that oversea
My kinsmen in their knighthood should lie dead,
Nor that this sudden death should set me free,
Me, the last Giustiniani—well, what then?
A monk!—The Giustiniani had been men.

So when the Abbot said: "The state decrees
That you, the latest scion of the house
Which died in vain for Venice overseas,
Should be exempted from your sacred vows,
And straightway, when you leave this cloistered place,
Take wife, and add new honors to the race,"

I hardly heard him—would have crept again
To the warped missal—but he snatched a sword
And girded me, and all the heart of men
Rushed through me, as he laughed and hailed me lord,
And, with my hand upon the hilt, I cried,
"Viva San Marco!" like my kin who died.

But, straightway, when, a new-made knight, I stood
Beneath the bridal arch, and saw you come,
A certain monkish warping of the blood
Ran up and struck the man's heart in me dumb;
I breathed an Ave to our Lady's grace,
And did not dare to look upon your face.

And when we swept the waters side by side,
With timbrelled gladness clashing on the air,
I trembled at your image in the tide,
And warded off the devil with a prayer,
Still seeming in a golden dream to move
Through fiendish labyrinths of forbidden love.

But when they left us, and we stood alone,
I, the last Giustiniani, face to face
With your unvisioned beauty, made my own
In this, the last strange bridal of our race,
And, looking up at last to meet your eyes,
Saw in their depths the star of love arise,

Ah, then the monk's garb shrivelled from my heart,
And left me man to face your womanhood.
Without a prayer to keep our lips apart
I turned about and kissed you where you stood,
And gathering all the gladness of my life
Into a new-found word, I called you "wife!"

EURYALUS

UPWARD we went by fields of asphodel,
Leaving Ortygia's moat-bound walls below;
By orchards, where the wind-flowers' drifted snow
Lay lightly heaped upon the turf's light swell;
By gardens, whence upon the wayside fell
Jasmine and rose in April's overflow;
Till, winding up in Epipolae's wide brow,
We reached at last the lonely citadel.

There, on the ruined rampart climbing high,
We sat and dreamed among the browsing sheep,
Until we heard the trumpet's startled cry
Waking a clang of arms about the keep,
And seaward saw, with rapt foreboding eye,
The sails of Athens whiten on the deep.

HAPPINESS

THIS perfect love can find no words to say.
What words are left, still sacred for our use,
That have not suffered the sad world's abuse,
And figure forth a gladness dimmed and gray?
Let us be silent still, since words convey
But shadowed images, wherein we lose
The fulness of love's light; our lips refuse
The fluent commonplace of yesterday.

Then shall we hear beneath the brooding wing
Of silence what abiding voices sleep,
The primal notes of nature, that outring
Man's little noises, warble he or weep,
The song the morning stars together sing,
The sound of deep that calleth unto deep.

BOTTICELLI'S MADONNA
IN THE LOUVRE

WHAT strange presentiment, O Mother, lies
On thy waste brow and sadly-folded lips,
Forefeeling the Light's terrible eclipse
On Calvary, as if love made thee wise,
And thou couldst read in those dear infant eyes
The sorrow that beneath their smiling sleeps,
And guess what bitter tears a mother weeps
When the cross darkens her unclouded skies?

Sad Lady, if some mother, passing thee,
Should feel a throb of thy foreboding pain,
And think—"My child at home clings so to me,
With the same smile . . . and yet in vain, in vain,
Since even this Jesus died on Calvary"—
Say to her then: "He also rose again."

THE SONNET

PURE form, that like some chalice of old time
Contain'st the liquid of the poet's thought
Within thy curving hollow, gem-enwrought
With interwoven traceries of rhyme,
While o'er thy brim the bubbling fancies climb,
What thing am I, that undismayed have sought
To pour my verse with trembling hand untaught
Into a shape so small yet so sublime?
Because perfection haunts the hearts of men,
Because thy sacred chalice gathered up
The wine of Petrarch, Shakspere, Shelley—then
Receive these tears of failure as they drop
(Sole vintage of my life), since I am fain
To pour them in a consecrated cup.

JADE

THE patient craftsman of the East who made
His undulant dragons of the veined jade,
And wound their sinuous volutes round the whole
Pellucid green redundance of the bowl,
Chiseled his subtle traceries with the same
Keen stone he wrought them in.
Nor praise, nor blame,
Nor gifts the years relinquish or refuse,
But only a grief commensurate with thy soul,
Shall carve it in a shape for gods to use.

PHAEDRA

NOT that on me the Cyprian fury fell,
Last martyr of my love-ensanguined race;
Not that my children drop the averted face
When my name shames the silence; not that hell
Holds me where nevermore his glance shall dwell
Nightlong between my lids, my pulses race
Through flying pines the tempest of the chase,
Nor my heart rest with him beside the well.

Not that he hates me; not, O baffled gods—
Not that I slew him!—yet, because your goal
Is always reached, nor your rejoicing rods
Fell ever yet upon insensate clods,
Know, the one pang that makes your triumph whole
Is, that he knows the baseness of my soul.

MOULD AND VASE

GREEK POTTERY OF AREZZO.

HERE in the jealous hollow of the mould,
Faint, light-eluding, as templed in the breast
Of some rose-vaulted lotus, see the best
The artist had—the vision that unrolled
Its flying sequence till completion's hold
Caught the wild round and bade the dancers rest—
The mortal lip on the immortal pressed
One instant, ere the blindness and the cold.

And there the vase: immobile, exiled, tame,
The captives of fulfillment link their round,
Foot-heavy on the inelastic ground,
How different, yet how enviously the same!
Dishonoring the kinship that they claim,
As here the written word the inner sound.

THE BREAD OF ANGELS

AT that lost hour disowned of day and night,
The after-birth of midnight, when life's face
Turns to the wall and the last lamp goes out
Before the incipient irony of dawn—
In that obliterate interval of time
Between the oil's last flicker and the first
Reluctant shudder of averted day,
Threading the city's streets (like mine own ghost
Wakening the echoes of dispeopled dreams),
I smiled to see how the last light that fought
Extinction was the old familiar glare
Of supper tables under gas-lit ceilings,
The same old stale monotonous carouse
Of greed and surfeit nodding face to face
O'er the picked bones of pleasure . . .
So that the city seemed, at that waste hour,
Like some expiring planet from whose face
All nobler life had perished—love and hate,
And labor and the ecstasy of thought—
Leaving the eyeless creatures of the ooze,
Dull offspring of its first inchoate birth,
The last to cling to its exhausted breast.

And threading thus the aimless streets that strayed
Conjectural through a labyrinth of death,
Strangely I came upon two hooded nuns,
Hands in their sleeves, heads bent as if beneath
Some weight of benediction, gliding by
Punctual as shadows that perform their round
Upon the inveterate bidding of the sun
Again and yet again their ordered course
At the same hour crossed mine: obedient shades
Cast by some high-orbed pity on the waste
Of midnight evil! and my wondering thoughts
Tracked them from the hushed convent where there kin
Lay hived in sweetness of their prayer built cells.
What wind of fate had loosed them from the lee
Of that dear anchorage where their sisters slept?
On what emprise of heavenly piracy

Did such frail craft put forth upon this world;
In what incalculable currents caught
And swept beyond the signal-lights of home
Did their white coifs set sail against the night?

At last, upon my wonder drawn, I followed
The secret wanderers till I saw them pause
Before the dying glare of those tall panes
Where greed and surfeit nodded face to face
O'er the picked bones of pleasure . . .
And the door opened and the nuns went in.

Again I met them, followed them again.
Straight as a thought of mercy to its goal
To the same door they sped. I stood alone.
And suddenly the silent city shook
With inarticulate clamor of gagged lips,
As in Jerusalem when the veil was rent
And the dead drove the living from the streets.
And all about me stalked the shrouded dead,
Dead hopes, dead efforts, loves and sorrows dead,
With empty orbits groping for their dead
In that blind mustering of murdered faiths . . .
And the door opened and the nuns came out.

I turned and followed. Once we came
To such a threshold, such a door received them,
They vanished, and I waited. The grim round
Ceased only when the festal panes grew dark
And the last door had shot its tardy bolt.
"Too late!" I heard one murmur; and "Too late!"
The other, in unholy antiphon.
And with dejected steps they turned away.

They turned, and still I tracked them, till they bent
Under the lee of a calm convent wall
Bounding a quiet street. I knew the street,
One of those village byways strangely trapped
In the city's meshes, where at loudest noon
The silence spreads like moss beneath the foot,
And all the tumult of the town becomes
Idle as Ocean's fury in a shell.

Silent at noon—but now, at this void hour,
When the blank sky hung over the blank streets
Clear as a mirror held above dead lips,
Came footfalls, and a thronging of dim shapes
About the convent door: a suppliant line
Of pallid figures, ghosts of happier folk,
Moving in some gray underworld of want
On which the sun of plenty never dawns.

And as the nuns approached I saw the throng
Pale emanation of that outcast hour,
Divide like vapor when the sun breaks through
And take the glory on its tattered edge.
For so a brightness ran from face to face,
Faint as a diver's light beneath the sea
And as a wave draws up the beach, the crowd
Drew to the nuns.
I waited. Then those two
Strange pilgrims of the sanctuaries of sin
Brought from beneath their large conniving cloaks
Two hidden baskets brimming with rich store
Of broken viands—pasties, jellies, meats,
Crumbs of Belshazzar's table, evil waste
Of that interminable nightly feast
Of greed and surfeit, nodding face to face
O'er the picked bones of pleasure . . .
And piteous hands were stretched to take the bread
Of this strange sacrament—this manna brought
Out of the antique wilderness of sin.

Each seized a portion, turning comforted
From this new breaking of the elements;
And while I watched the mystery of renewal
Whereby the dead bones of old sins become
The living body of the love of God,
It seemed to me that a like change transformed
The city's self . . . a little wandering air
Ruffled the ivy on the convent wall;
A bird piped doubtfully; the dawn replied;
And in that ancient gray necropolis
Somewhere a child awoke and took the breast.

OGRIN THE HERMIT

Vous qui nous jugez, savez-vous quel boivre nous avons bu sûr la mer?

> *Ogrin the Hermit in old age set forth*
> *This tale to them that sought him in the extreme*
> *Ancient grey wood where he and silence housed:*

Long years ago, when yet my sight was keen,
My hearing knew the word of wind in bough,
And all the low fore-runners of the storm,
There reached me, where I sat beneath my thatch,
A crash as of tracked quarry in the brake,
And storm-flecked, fugitive, with straining breasts
And backward eyes and hands inseparable,
Tristan and Iseult, swooning at my feet,
Sought hiding from their hunters. Here they lay.

For pity of their great extremity,
Their sin abhorring, yet not them with it,
I nourished, hid, and suffered them to build
Their branched hut in sight of this grey cross,
That haply, falling on their guilty sleep,
Its shadow should part them like the blade of God,
And they should shudder at each other's eyes.

So dwelt they in this solitude with me,
And daily, Tristan forth upon the chase,
The tender Iseult sought my door and heard
The words of holiness. Abashed she heard,
Like one in wisdom nurtured from a child,
Yet in whose ears an alien language dwells
Of some far country whence the traveller brings
Magical treasure, and still images
Of gods forgotten, and the scent of groves
That sleep by painted rivers. As I have seen
Oft-times returning pilgrims with the spell
Of these lost lands upon their lids, she moved
Among familiar truths, accustomed sights,
As she to them were strange, not they to her.
And often, reasoning with her, have I felt

Some ancient lore was in her, dimly drawn
From springs of life beyond the four-fold stream
That makes a silver pale to Paradise;
For she was calm as some forsaken god
Who knows not that his power is passed from him,
But sees with tranced eyes rich pilgrim-trains
In sands the desert blows about his feet.

Abhorring first, I heard her; yet her speech
Warred not with pity, or the contrite heart,
Or hatred of things evil: rather seemed
The utterance of some world where these are not,
And the heart lives in heathen innocence
With earth's innocuous creatures. For she said:
"Love is not, as the shallow adage goes,
A witch's filter, brewed to trick the blood.
The cup we drank of on the flying deck
Was the blue vault of air, the round world's lip,
Brimmed with life's hydromel, and pressed to ours
By myriad hands of wind and sun and sea.
For these are all the cup-bearers of youth,
That bend above it at the board of life,
Solicitous accomplices: there's not
A leaf on bough, a foam-flash on the wave,
So brief and glancing but it serves them too;
No scent the pale rose spends upon the night,
Nor sky-lark's rapture trusted to the blue,
But these, from the remotest tides of air
Brought in mysterious salvage, breathe and sing
In lovers' lips and eyes; and two that drink
Thus onely of the strange commingled cup
Of mortal fortune shall into their blood
Take magic gifts. Upon each others' hearts
They shall surprise the heart-beat of the world,
And feel a sense of life in things inert;
For as love's touch upon the yielded body
Is a diviner's wand, and where it falls
A hidden treasure trembles: so their eyes,
Falling upon the world of clod and brute,
And cold hearts plotting evil, shall discern
The inextinguishable flame of life
That girdles the remotest frame of things

With influences older than the stars."

So spake Iseult; and thus her passion found
Far-flying words, like birds against the sunset
That look on lands we see not. Yet I know
It was not any argument she found,
But that she was, the colour that life took
About her, that thus reasoned in her stead,
Making her like a lifted lantern borne
Through midnight thickets, where the flitting ray
Momently from inscrutable darkness draws
A myriad-veined branch, and its shy nest
Quivering with startled life: so moved Iseult.
And all about her this deep solitude
Stirred with responsive motions. Oft I knelt
In night-long vigil while the lovers slept
Under their outlawed thatch, and with long prayers
Sought to disarm the indignant heavens; but lo,
Thus kneeling in the intertidal hour
'Twixt dark and dawning, have mine eyes beheld
How the old gods that hide in these hoar woods,
And were to me but shapings of the air,
And flit and murmur of the breathing trees,
Or slant of moon on pools—how these stole forth,
Grown living presences, yet not of bale,
But innocent-eyed as fawns that come to drink,
Thronging the threshold where the lovers lay,
In service of the great god housed within
Who hides in his breast, beneath his mighty plumes,
The purposes and penalties of life.
Or in yet deeper hours, when all was still,
And the hushed air bowed over them alone,
Such music of the heart as lovers hear,
When close as lips lean, lean the thoughts between—
When the cold world, no more a lonely orb
Circling the unimagined track of Time,
Is like a beating heart within their hands,
A numb bird that they warm, and feel its wings—
Such music have I heard; and through the prayers
Wherewith I sought to shackle their desires,
And bring them humbled to the feet of God,
Caught the loud quiring of the fruitful year,

The leap of springs, the throb of loosened earth,
And the sound of all the streams that seek the sea.

So fell it, that when pity moved their hearts,
And those high lovers, one unto the end,
Bowed to the sundering will, and each his way
Went through a world that could not make them twain,
Knowing that a great vision, passing by,
Had swept mine eye-lids with its fringe of fire,
I, with the wonder of it on my head,
And with the silence of it in my heart,
Forth to Tintagel went by secret ways,
A long lone journey; and from them that loose
Their spiced bales upon the wharves, and shake
Strange silks to the sun, or covertly unbosom
Rich hoard of pearls and amber, or let drip
Through swarthy fingers links of sinuous gold,
Chose their most delicate treasures. Though I knew
No touch more silken than this knotted gown,
My hands, grown tender with the sense of her,
Discerned the airiest tissues, light to cling
As shower-loosed petals, veils like meadow-smoke,
Fur soft as snow, amber like sun congealed,
Pearls pink as may-buds in an orb of dew;
And laden with these wonders, that to her
Were natural as the vesture of a flower,
Fared home to lay my booty at her feet.

And she, consenting, nor with useless words
Proving my purpose, robed herself therein
To meet her lawful lord; but while she thus
Prisoned the wandering glory of her hair,
Dimmed her bright breast with jewels, and subdued
Her light to those dull splendours, well she knew
The lord that I adorned her thus to meet
Was not Tintagel's shadowy King, but he,
That other lord beneath whose plumy feet
The currents of the seas of life run gold
As from eternal sunrise; well she knew
That when I laid my hands upon her head,
Saying, "Fare forth forgiven," the words I spoke
Were the breathings of his pity, who beholds

How, swept on his inexorable wings
Too far beyond the planetary fires
On the last coasts of darkness, plunged too deep
In light ineffable, the heart amazed
Swoons of its glory, and dropping back to earth
Craves the dim shelter of familiar sounds,
The rain on the roof, the noise of flocks that pass,
And the slow world waking to its daily round. . . .

And thus, as one who speeds a banished queen,
I set her on my mule, and hung about
With royal ornament she went her way;
For meet it was that this great Queen should pass
Crowned and forgiven from the face of Love.

THE COMRADE

WILD winged thing, O brought I know not whence
To beat your life out in my life's low cage;
You strange familiar, nearer than my flesh
Yet distant as a star, that were at first
A child with me a child, yet elfin-far,
And visibly of some unearthly breed;
Mirthfullest mate of all my mortal games,
Yet shedding on them some evasive gleam
Of Latmian loneliness—O seven then
Expert to lift the latch of our low door
And profit by the hours when, dusked about
By human misintelligence, our first
Weak fledgling flights were safeliest essayed;
Divine accomplice of those perilous-sweet
Low moth-flights of the unadventured soul
Above the world's dim garden!—now we sit,
After what stretch of years, what stretch of wings,
In the same cage together—still as near
And still as strange!
Only I know at last
That we are fellows till the last night falls,
And that I shall not miss your comrade hands
Till they have closed my lids, and by them set
A taper that—who knows!—may yet shine through.

Sister, my comrade, I have ached for you,
Sometimes, to see you curb your pace to mine,
And bow your Maenad crest to the dull forms
Of human usage; I have loosed your hand
And whispered: 'Go! Since I am tethered here;'
And you have turned, and breathing for reply,
'I too am pinioned, as you too are free,'
Have caught me to such undreamed distances
As the last planets see, when they look forth,
To the sentinel pacings of the outmost stars—
Nor these alone,
Comrade, my sister, were your gifts. More oft
Has your impalpable wing-brush bared for me
The heart of wonder in familiar things,

Unroofed dull rooms, and hung above my head
The cloudy glimpses of a vernal moon,
Or all the autumn heaven ripe with stars.

And you have made a secret pact with Sleep,
And when she comes not, or her feet delay,
Toiled in low meadows of gray asphodel
Under a pale sky where no shadows fall,
Then, hooded like her, to my side you steal,
And the night grows like a great rumouring sea,
And you a boat, and I your passenger,
And the tide lifts us with an indrawn breath
Out, out upon the murmurs and the scents,
Through spray of splintered star-beams, or white rage
Of desperate moon-drawn waters—on and on
To some blue ocean immarcescible
That ever like a slow-swung mirror rocks
The balanced breasts of sea-birds motionless.

Yet other nights, my sister, you have been
The storm, and I the leaf that fled on it
Terrifically down voids that never knew
The pity of creation—or have felt
The immitigable anguish of a soul
Left last in a long-ruined world alone;
And then your touch has drawn me back to earth,
As in the night, upon an unknown road,
A scent of lilac breathing from the hedge
Bespeaks the hidden farm, the bedded cows,
And safety, and the sense of human kind . . .

And I have climbed with you by hidden ways
To meet the dews of morning, and have seen
The shy gods like retreating shadows fade,
Or on the thymy reaches have surprised
Old Chiron sleeping, and have waked him not . . .

Yet farther have I fared with you, and known
Love and his sacred tremors, and the rites
Of his most inward temple; and beyond
His temple lights, have seen the long gray waste
Where lonely thoughts, like creatures of the night,

Listen and wander where a city stood.
And creeping down by waterless defiles
Under an iron midnight, have I kept
My vigil in the waste till dawn began
To move among the ruins, and I saw
A sapling rooted in a fissured plinth,
And a wren's nest in the thunder-threatening hand
Of some old god of granite in the dust . . .

SUMMER AFTERNOON
(Bodiam Castle, Sussex)

NOT all the wasteful beauty of the year
Heaped in the scale of one consummate hour
Shall this outweigh: the curve of quiet air
That held, as in the green sun-fluted light
Of sea-caves quivering in a tidal lull,
Those tranced towers and long unruined walls,
Moat-girdled from the world's dissolving touch,
The rook-flights lessening over evening woods,
And, down the unfrequented grassy slopes,
The shadows of old oaks contemplative
Reaching behind them like the thoughts of age.

High overhead hung the long Sussex ridge,
Sun-cinctured, as a beaker's rim of gold
Curves round its green concavity; and slow
Across the upper pastures of the sky
The clouds moved white before the herding airs
That in the hollow, by the moated walls,
Stirred not one sleeping lily from its sleep.

Deeper the hush fell; more remote the earth
Fled onward with the flight of cloud and sun,
And cities strung upon the flashing reel
Of nights and days. We knew no more of these
Than the grey towers redoubling in the moat
The image of a bygone strength transformed
To beauty's endless uses; and like them
We felt the touch of that renewing power
That turns the landmarks of man's ruined toil
To high star-haunted reservoirs of peace.
And with that sense there came the deeper sense
Of moments that, between the beats of time,
May thus insphere in some transcendent air
The plenitude of being.
Far currents feed them, from those slopes of soul

That know the rise and set of other stars
White-roaring downward through remote defiles
Dim-forested with unexplored thought;
Yet tawny from the flow of lower streams
That drink the blood of battle, sweat of earth,
And the broached vats of cities revelling.
All these the moments hold; yet these resolved
To such clear wine of beauty as shall flush
The blood to richer living. . . . Thus we mused,
And musing thus we felt the magic touch,
And such a moment held us. As, at times,
Through the long windings of each other's eyes
We have reached some secret hallowed silent place
That a god visits at the turn of night—
In such a solitude the moment held us.
And one were thought and sense in that profound
Submersion of all being deep below
The vexed waves of action. Clear we saw,
Through the clear nether stillness of the place,
The gliding images of words and looks
Swept from us down the gusty tides of time,
And here unfolding to completer life;
And like dull pebbles from a sunless shore
Plunged into crystal waters, suddenly
We took the hues of beauty, and became,
Each to the other, all that each had sought.

Thus did we feel the moment and the place
One in the heart of beauty; while far off
The rooks' last cry died on the fading air,
And the first star stood white upon the hill.

POMEGRANATE SEED

DEMETER PERSEPHONE
HECATE HERMES
In the vale of Elusis

DEMETER

Hail, goddess, from the midmost caverned vale
Of Samothracia, where with darksome rites
Unnameable, and sacrificial lambs,
Pale priests salute thy triple-headed form,
Borne hither by swift Hermes o'er the sea:
Hail, Hecate, what word soe'er thou bring
To me, undaughtered, of my vanished child.

HECATE

Word have I, but no Samothracian wild
Last saw me, and mine aged footsteps pine
For the bleak vale, my dusky-pillared house,
And the cold murmur of incessant rites
Forever falling down mine altar-steps
Into black pools of fear . . . for I am come
Even now from that blue-cinctured westward isle,
Trinacria, where, till thou withheldst thy face,
Yearly three harvests yellowed to the sun,
And vines deep-laden yoked the heavier boughs—
Trinacria, that last saw Persephone.

DEMETER

Now, triune goddess, may the black ewe-lambs
Pour a red river down thine altar-steps,
Fruit, loaves and honey, at the cross-roads laid,
With each young moon by pious hands renewed,
Appease thee, and the Thracian vale resound
With awful homage to thine oracle!
What bring'st thou of Persephone, my child?

HECATE

Thy daughter lives, yet never sees the sun.

DEMETER

Blind am I in her blindness. Tell no more.

HECATE

Blind is she not, and yet beholds no light.

DEMETER

Dark as her doom is, are thy words to me.

HECATE

When the wild chariot of the flying sea
Bore me to Etna, 'neath his silver slope
Herding their father's flocks three maids I found,
The daughters of the god whose golden house
Rears in the east its cloudy peristyle.
"Helios, our father," to my quest they cried,
"Was last to see Persephone on earth."

DEMETER

On earth? What nameless region holds her now?

HECATE

Even as I put thy question to the three,
Etna became as one who knows a god,
And wondrously, across the waiting deep,
Wave after wave the golden portent bore,
Till Helios rose before us.

DEMETER

O, I need
Thy words as the parched valleys need my rain!

HECATE

May the draught slake thee! Thus the god replied:
When the first suns of March with verdant flame
Relume the fig-trees in the crannied hills,
And the pale myrtle scents the rain-washed air—
Ere oleanders down the mountain stream
Pass the wild torch of summer, and my kine

Breathe of gold gorse and honey-laden sage;
Between the first white flowering of the bay
And the last almond's fading from the hill,
Along the fields of Enna came a maid
Who seemed among her mates to move alone,
As the full moon will mow the sky of stars,
And whom, by that transcendence, I divined
Of breed Olympian, and Demeter's child.

DEMETER

All-seeing god! So walks she in my dreams.

HECATE

Persephone (so spake the god of day)
Ran here and there with footsteps that out-shone
The daffodils she gathered, while her maids,
Like shadows of herself by noon fore-shortened,
On every side her laughing task prolonged;
When suddenly the warm and trusted earth
Widened black jaws beneath them, and therefrom
Rose Aides, whom with averted head
Pale mortals worship, as the poplar turns,
Whitening, her fearful foliage from the gale.
Like thunder rolling up against the wind
He dusked the sky with midnight ere he came,
Whirling his cloak of subterraneous cloud
In awful coils about the fated maid,
Till nothing marked the place where she had stood
But her dropped flowers—a garland on a grave.

DEMETER

Where is that grave? There will I lay me down,
And know no more the change of night to day.

HECATE

Such is the cry that mortal mothers make;
But the sun rises, and their task goes on.

DEMETER

Yet happier they, that make an end at last.

HECATE

Behold, along the Eleusinian vale
A god approaches, by his feathered tread
Arcadian Hermes. Wait upon his word.

DEMETER

I am a god. What do the gods avail?

HECATE

Oft have I heard that cry—but not the answer.

HERMES

Demeter, from Olympus am I come,
By laurelled Tempe and Thessalian ways,
Charged with grave words of aegis-bearing Zeus.

DEMETER

(*as if she has not heard him*)
If there be any grief I have not borne,
Go, bring it here, and I will give it suck . . .

HERMES

Thou art a god, and speakest mortal words?

DEMETER

Even the gods grow greater when they love.

HERMES

It is the Life-giver who speaks by me.

DEMETER

I want no words but those my child shall speak.

HERMES

His words are winged seeds that carry hope
To root and ripen in long-barren hearts.

DEMETER

Deeds, and not words, alone can quicken me.

HERMES

His words are fruitfuller than deeds of men.
Why hast thou left Olympus, and thy kind?

DEMETER

Because my kind are they that walk the earth
For numbered days, and lay them down in graves.
My sisters are the miserable women
Who seek their children up and down the world,
Who feel a babe's hand at the faded breast,
And live upon the words of lips gone dumb.
Sorrow no footing on Olympus finds,
And the gods are gods because their hearts forget.

HERMES

Why then, since thou hast cast thy lot with those
Who painfully endure vain days on earth,
Hast thou, harsh arbitress of fruit and flower,
Cut off the natural increase of the fields?
The baffled herds, tongues lolling, eyes agape,
Range wretchedly from sullen spring to spring,
A million sun-blades lacerate the ground,
And the shrunk fruits untimely drop, like tears
That Earth at her own desolation sheds.
These are the words Zeus bids me bring to thee.

DEMETER

To whom reply: No pasture longs for rain
As for Persephone I thirst and hunger.
Give me my child, and all the earth shall laugh
Like Rhodian rose-fields in the eye of June.

HERMES

What if such might were mine? What if, indeed,
The exorable god, thy pledge confirmed,
Should yield thee back the daughter of thy tears?

DEMETER

Such might is thine?
Beyond Cithaeron, see
The footsteps of the rain upon the hills.

HERMES

Tell me whence thy daughter must be led.

HECATE

So much at least it shall be mine to do.
If ever urgency hath plumed thy heels,
By Psyttaleia and the outer isles
Westward still winging thine ethereal way,
Beyond the moon-swayed reaches of the deep,
And that unvestiged midnight that confines
The verge of being, succourable god,
Haste to the river by whose sunless brim
Dark Aides leads forth his languid flocks.
There shalt thou find Persephone enthroned.
Beside the ruler of the dead she sits,
And shares, unwilling, his long sovereignty.
Thence lead her to Demeter and these groves.

DEMETER

Round thy returning feet the earth shall laugh
As I, when of my body she was born!

HECATE

Lo, thy last word is as a tardy shaft
Lost in his silver furrow. Ere thou speed
Its fellow, we shall see his face again
And not alone. The gods are justified.

DEMETER

Ah, how impetuous are the wings of joy!
Swift comes she, as impatient to be gone!
Swifter than yonder rain moves down the pass
I see the wonder run along the deep.
The light draws nearer. . . . Speak to me, my child!

HECATE

I feel the first slow rain-drop on my hand . . .
She fades. Persephone comes, led by Hermes.

PERSEPHONE

How sweet the hawthorn smells along the hedge . . .
And, mother, mother, sweeter are these tears.

DEMETER

Pale art thou, daughter, and upon thy brow
Sits an estranging darkness like a crown.
Look up, look up! Drink in the light's new wine.
Feelest thou not beneath thine alien feet
Earth's old endearment, O Persephone?

PERSEPHONE

Dear is the earth's warm pressure under foot,
And dear, my mother, is thy hand in mine.
As one who, prisoned in some Asian wild,
After long days of cheated wandering
Climbing a sudden cliff, at last beholds
The boundless reassurance of the sea,
And on it one small sail that sets for home,
So look I on the daylight, and thine eyes.

DEMETER

Thy voice is paler than the lips it leaves.
Thou wilt not stay with me! I know my doom.

PERSEPHONE

Ah, the sweet rain! The clouds compassionate!
Hide me, O mother, hide me from the day!

DEMETER

What are these words? It is my love thou fearest.

PERSEPHONE

I fear the light. I fear the sound of life
That thunders in mine unaccustomed ears.

DEMETER

Here is no sound but the soft-falling rain.

PERSEPHONE

Dost thou not hear the noise of birth and being,
The roar of sap in boughs impregnated,
And all the deafening rumour of the grass?

DEMETER

Love hear I, at his endless task of life.

PERSEPHONE

The awful immortality of life!
The white path winding deathlessly to death!
Why didst thou call the rain from out her caves
To draw a dying earth back to the day?
Why fatten flocks for our dark feast, who sit
Beside the gate, and know where the path ends?
O pitiless gods—that I am one of you!

DEMETER

They are not pitiless, since thou art here.

PERSEPHONE

Who am I, that they give me, or withhold?
Think'st thou I am that same Persephone
They took from thee?

DEMETER

Within thine eyes I see
Some dreadful thing—

PERSEPHONE

At first I deemed it so.

DEMETER

Loving thy doom, more dark thou mak'st it seem.

PERSEPHONE

Love? What is love? This long time I've unlearned
Those old unquiet words. There where we sit,
By the sad river of the end, still are
The poplars, still the shaken hearts of men,
Or if they stir, it is as when in sleep
Dogs sob upon a phantom quarry's trail.
And ever through their listlessness there runs
The lust of some old anguish; never yet
Hath any asked for happiness: that gift
They fear too much! But they would sweat and strive,
And clear a field, or kill a man, or even
Wait on some long slow vengeance all their days.

DEMETER

Since I have sat upon the stone of sorrow,
Think'st thou I know not how the dead may feel?
But thou, look up; for thou shalt learn from me,
Under the sweet day, in the paths of men,
All the dear human offices that make
Their brief hour longer than the years of death.
Thou shalt behold me wake the sleeping seed,
And wing the flails upon the threshing-floor,
Among young men and maidens; or at dawn,
Under the low thatch, in the winnowing-creel,
Lay the new infant, seedling of some warm
Noon dalliance in the golden granary,
Who shall in turn rise, walk, and drive the plough,
And in the mortal furrow leave his seed.

PERSEPHONE

Execrable offices are theirs and thine!
Mine only nurslings are the waxen-pale
Dead babes, so small that they are hard to tell
>From the little images their mothers lay
Beside them, that they may not sleep alone.

DEMETER

Yet other nurslings to those mothers come,
And live and love—

PERSEPHONE

Thou hast not seen them meet,
Ghosts of dead babes and ghosts of tired men,
Or thou wouldst veil thy face, and curse the sun!

DEMETER

Thou wilt forget the things that thou hast seen.

PERSEPHONE

More dreadful are the things thou hast to show.

DEMETER

Art thou so certain? Hard is it for men
To know a god, and it has come to me
That we, we also, may be blind to men.

PERSEPHONE

O mother, thou hast spoken! But for me,
I, that have eaten of the seed of death,
And with my dead die daily, am become
Of their undying kindred, and no more
Can sit within the doorway of the gods
And laughing spin new souls along the years.

DEMETER

Daughter, speak low. Since I have walked with men
Olympus is a little hill, no more.
Stay with me on the dear and ample earth.

PERSEPHONE

The kingdom of the dead is wider still,
And there I heal the wounds that thou hast made.

DEMETER

And yet I send thee beautiful ghosts and griefs!
Dispeopling earth, I leave thee none to rule.

PERSEPHONE

O that, mine office ended, I might end!

DEMETER

Stand off from me. Thou knowest more than I,
Who am but the servant of some lonely will.

PERSEPHONE

Perchance the same. But me it calls from hence.

DEMETER

On earth, on earth, thou wouldst have wounds to heal!

PERSEPHONE

Free me. I hear the voices of my dead.
She goes.

DEMETER

(after a long silence)
I hear the secret whisper of the wheat.